CHAOS AND TEMPTATIONS

CHAOS AND TEMPTATIONS

BRITTANY HOBBS

publisher logo

Contents

1

CHAOS AND TEMPTATIONS

MY FATHER'S JOURNEY TO REDEMPTION
BRITTANY HOBBS

2

First Edition 2024

Published by Brittany Hobbs

3

CONTENTS

INTRODUCTION

INTRODUCTION

Amidst the tumultuous waves of life, the story of my father's pursuit of redemption unfolds with raw, unfiltered honesty. His path was never linear; it was marred by unpredictability and fraught with temptations that threatened to derail him at every turn. This narrative is not merely an account of his struggles, but a testament to the human spirit's resilience and capacity for transformation.

From the earliest days of his youth, my father was ensnared by the allure of chaos. It wasn't that he sought out trouble; rather, trouble seemed to find him, lurking in the shadows of his choices and the company he kept. As he navigated the labyrinth of his existence, he encountered moments of profound darkness, where the glimmer of hope seemed all but extinguished. Yet, within him burned an unyielding desire for something more—a life of meaning, peace, and ultimately, forgiveness.

This book delves into the intricate layers of his experiences, peeling back the veneer of a man who, for much of his life, was a mystery even to those closest to him. Through a series of poignant recollections, personal reflections, and candid revelations, we come to understand the forces that shaped him, the demons he battled, and the moments of grace that offered him a lifeline.

In tracing the contours of his journey, we witness the profound impact of familial bonds, the redemptive power of love, and the significance of second chances. My father's story is not one of instant redemption, but of gradual awakening—an awakening to his own potential for goodness and the realization that true change requires both time and unwavering commitment.

This is a story for those who have ever felt lost, for those who have wrestled with their own imperfections, and for those who believe in the possibility of redemption, no matter how far one has strayed. As we walk alongside my father through the pages of this book, we are reminded that the path to redemption is seldom straight, but it is always within reach for those who dare to seek it.

5

Chapter 1: Early Years

Small Town Beginnings

Nestled in the heart of the Midwest, the small town of Millfield exuded an air of tranquility and simplicity. With a population barely scraping past two thousand, it was the kind of place where everyone knew everyone else, and news traveled faster than the morning paper. The town's layout was straightforward: a single main street lined with mom-and-pop shops, a solitary diner, a modest library, and a town hall that doubled as a community center.

Millfield's history was etched in its architecture. The buildings, mostly constructed in the early 20th century, bore the charm of a bygone era. Red-brick facades, white picket fences, and wooden shutters painted in pastel hues gave the town a postcard-perfect appearance. The local school, an old brick structure with ivy creeping up its walls, was a testament to the town's enduring legacy. Generations of Millfield's residents had walked through its halls, their lives intertwined with the institution's history.

The town's economy revolved around agriculture. Rolling fields of corn and wheat stretched out as far as the eye could see, punctuated by the occasional barn or silo. The farmers, resilient and hardworking, formed the backbone of the community. Their routines were dictated by the seasons, a rhythm that the town had come to respect and depend upon. During harvest time, the entire community came together, lending a hand in the fields and celebrating the bounty with communal feasts.

Traditions played a significant role in Millfield's social fabric. Annual events like the county fair, the harvest festival, and the winter carnival were eagerly anticipated. These gatherings were more than just social events; they were the glue that held the community together. The county fair, with its pie-baking contests, livestock shows, and merry-go-round, was a highlight of the summer. The harvest festival, marked by a parade of tractors and floats, celebrated the end of the growing season. The winter carnival, with its ice-skating rink and hot cocoa stands, brought warmth and cheer to the cold months.

Despite its idyllic appearance, Millfield was not without its challenges. The younger generation, lured by the promise of opportunities in the cities, often left for college and did not return. This exodus left behind an aging population and a sense of nostalgia for the bustling town it once was. The local businesses, though cherished by the community, struggled to compete with the convenience of online shopping and big-box retailers in nearby towns.

However, Millfield's residents were nothing if not resilient. The town had weathered economic downturns, natural disasters, and societal changes with a steadfast determination. The spirit of cooperation and mutual support was deeply ingrained in the community. Neighbors looked out for one another, and the concept of lending a helping hand was not just a saying but a way of life.

In the midst of this setting, the story of Chaos and Temptations unfolds. Against the backdrop of a town steeped in tradition and simplicity, the characters' lives are set to intersect in ways that will challenge their perceptions and test their resolve. The seemingly placid exterior of Millfield belies the undercurrents of ambition, desire, and conflict that simmer beneath the surface. As the narrative progresses, the town's quiet charm will serve as both a haven and a crucible for the unfolding drama.

6

❧

Your Demo Book's First Subchapter is Complete!
Ready for More? Finish This Book or Start a New One!
Steps to Proceed:

- **Buy Credits:** Choose and purchase a <u>Credit Package</u>.
- **Finish This Book:** Click the "Finish the Book" button on <u>My Books</u> page to complete it.
- **Start a New Book:** For a different topic, click the "Create A Book" after buying credits.

Action Needed:
<u>Purchase Credits Here</u>
Need Help?
Contact our support team <u>here</u>.
Explore. Learn. Create.
Thank you for trying our Demo Book. Let's continue the journey together.

Early Mischief

Joyride Gone Wrong

A Forbidden Love

Starting a Family

7

Chapter 2: Struggles and Survival

Living with Parents

Financial Hardships

First Christmas

Turning to Marijuana

A Growing Family

8

Chapter 3: Escaping the Past

Old Habits

Legal Troubles

Seeking Redemption

Community Service

A New Beginning

9

Chapter 4: Temptations Resurface

Old Friends

The Lure of Easy Money

Family Tensions

Moral Dilemmas

A Critical Choice

10

Chapter 5: A Father's Love

Bonding with Daughters

Lessons Learned

Protecting the Family

Sacrifices Made

A Promise to Change

11

Chapter 6: The Road to Redemption

Seeking Help

Rebuilding Trust

Facing the Past

Making Amends

Steps Forward

12

Chapter 7: Challenges and Setbacks

Relapse

Family Struggles

Financial Pressure

Health Issues

Finding Strength

13

Chapter 8: Support Networks

Friends and Allies

Community Support

Family Bonds

Professional Help

A United Front

14

Chapter 9: Personal Growth

Self-Reflection

New Hobbies

Educational Pursuits

Spiritual Journey

A Changed Man

15

Chapter 10: Reconnecting with the Past

Old Acquaintances

Family Reunions

Revisiting Old Haunts

Lessons from the Past

Moving Forward

16

Chapter 11: Building a Future

Career Changes

Financial Planning

Investing in Family

Home Improvements

A Brighter Tomorrow

17

Chapter 12: Facing New Temptations

Modern Challenges

Digital Age Temptations

Balancing Work and Life

Maintaining Sobriety

Family First

18

Chapter 13: Community Involvement

Volunteering

Mentoring Others

Local Projects

Giving Back

Leaving a Legacy

19

Chapter 14: Reflections and Realizations

Looking Back

Lessons Learned

Family Insights

Personal Achievements

Contentment

20

Chapter 15: A New Dawn

Future Aspirations

Family Goals

Continued Growth

Embracing Change

A Promising Future